Radio Waves

Tom Easton and Sophie Escabasse

WAYLAND

www.waylandbooks.co.uk

Miss Collins is the Careers Officer.
She's been fixing up work
experience for me.

"Hello, Dan," she said. "What can I do for you?"

"Err…" I said. "Have you got any new jobs?"

On her desk Miss Collins had a box.
In the box were cards with lists
of all the jobs. She picked out a card.
 "There is one job," she said.

Then she stopped and frowned.

"Go on," I said. "What is it? A test pilot? A football commentator?"

Of course it wasn't.

But it was almost as good.

It was a job at the radio station.

My boss at the radio station was
called Ryan. He had strange hair.
He had strange glasses.
I tried not to stare.

My new job was going to be brilliant.
I would play records and talk to callers.
Soon they would be calling it
'The Dan Show'.

Then Ryan handed me a mop.

"What's this?" I asked.

"It's a mop," said Ryan.

"Get cleaning!"

Oh well, I thought. Everyone has to start at the bottom. But it wasn't just mopping. I had to dust, polish, wipe and scrub. It was really hard work!

As I worked, I looked around.
I could see through the window
into the studio. I could see Ryan
at the microphone.

Ryan was playing an awful song. Then he spoke into the microphone.

"That was Baby Blue by the Blue Babies. One of my all-time favourites," he said. Ryan's voice was really squeaky. I burst out laughing.

"I could do better than Ryan,"
I thought. I carried on mopping.

I went into an empty studio to clean it.

I was quite tired. I sat down for a rest.

"I wonder what that button does?"

I thought.

I may have pressed one or two buttons. I may even have turned a knob.

The next thing I knew there was
music playing. It was good music too.
Better than the Blue Babies.

I sang along,
making up the words.

"Ryan plays such rubbish tunes,
His glasses make him look a fool,
Everyone just stops and stares,
At Ryan's really stupid hair."

21

I grabbed the mop.

I pretended it was a guitar.

I spun around. I was so cool.

I could see some people at the studio
window. They waved at me.
I waved back.

Then Ryan rushed into the room.
He pressed a button. The music
stopped. He looked very angry.

"You were on-air!" he shouted.
"All our listeners could hear you!"

25

Then I remembered what
I had been singing. Oops!
"Now you tell me! I didn't
know that was the On-air
button," I said.

"You shouldn't have pressed any buttons!" screamed Ryan. "Get out of here now!"

Ryan looked like he might cry. I thought I had better go. Maybe radio wasn't the right job for me.

"I wonder if Miss Collins has any jobs in TV for me?" I thought.

Read more stories about Dan.

978 0 7502 8228 4

Dan's latest work experience is at a car yard. All Dan has to do is sell a car. What could possibly go wrong?

978 0 7502 8225 3

Dan's latest work experience is as a grave digger. All Dan has to do is dig a hole. What could possibly go wrong?

978 0 7502 8226 0

Dan's latest work experience is at a flower shop. All Dan has to do is deliver flowers on Valentine's Day. What could possibly go wrong?

Read some more books
in the Freestylers series.

FOOTBALL FACTOR

Each story follows the ups
and downs of one member
of the football team Sheldon
Rovers as they aim for
Cup glory.

978 0 7502 7985 7

978 0 7502 7980 2

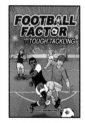

978 0 7502 7982 6

978 0 7502 7984 0

978 0 7502 7981 9

978 0 7502 7983 3

SHORT THRILLERS

Cool crime detectives, Jas and Sam, solve spine-chilling
cases with humour and bravery.

978 0 7502 6895 0

978 0 7502 6896 7

978 0 7502 6898 1

978 0 7502 6897 4

FOR TEACHERS

About
Freestylers

Freestylers is a series of carefully levelled stories, especially geared for struggling readers. With very low reading age and high interest age, these books are humorous, fun, up-to-the-minute and edgy. Core characters provide familiarity in all of the stories, build confidence and ease pupils from one story through to the next, accelerating reading progress.

Freestylers can be used for both guided and independent reading. To make the most of the books you can:

- Focus on making each reading session successful. Talk about the text before the pupil starts reading. Introduce the characters, the storyline and any unfamiliar vocabulary.

- Encourage the pupil to talk about the book during reading and after reading. How would they have felt if they were one of the characters? How would they have dealt with the situations that Dan found himself in?

- Talk about which parts of the story they like best and why.

For guidance, this story has been approximately measured to:

National Curriculum Level: 2B
Reading Age: 6
Book Band: Orange

ATOS: 1.9
Lexile ® Measure [confirmed]: 210L